**BLM Technical Note 435**

# Accipiter Use of Pinyon–Juniper Habitats for Nesting in Northwestern Colorado

Steven J. Slater and Jeff P. Smith[1]

HawkWatch International, Inc.
2240 South 900 East
Salt Lake City, Utah 84106

[1] Phone: (801) 484-6808 x109
Email: jsmith@hawkwatch.org

Prepared for:
U.S. Department of Interior,
Bureau of Land Management
Utah State Office, Salt Lake City,
Wyoming State Office, Cheyenne, and
Colorado State Office, Lakewood

# Table of Contents

# List of Tables

Although substantial research has been directed at understanding accipiter nesting-habitat relationships, little attention has been paid to pinyon–juniper (*Pinus edulis* or *monophylla – Juniperus* spp.) vegetation of the western United States. Previous surveys conducted by the Bureau of Land Management (BLM) in northwestern Colorado suggested that accipiter nesting in these habitats might be more common than previously acknowledged, leading to a BLM-sponsored study of this phenomenon by HawkWatch International in the Piceance Basin of Colorado. Broadcast surveys and nest searches suggested that in 2007 there were a minimum of 0–2 Sharp-shinned Hawk (*Accipiter striatus*), 13–29 Cooper's Hawk (*A. cooperii*), and 3–6 Northern Goshawk (*A. gentilis*) nests active in the study area. Although we did not design our surveys to produce robust estimates of nesting density, spacing of active nests located between 2005 and 2007 suggested that all three accipiters probably occur at relatively low densities in pinyon-juniper habitat in the study area compared to estimates derived from studies in other regions and vegetation types. Vegetation surveys also suggested that Sharp-shinned Hawk (*n* = 3) nest sites contained smaller trees and a greater density of small trees compared to the other two accipiters. Cooper's Hawk (*n* = 10) and Northern Goshawk (*n* = 10) nest and nest-site characteristics overlapped considerably. All of the surveyed accipiter nests that we found were on northwestern through eastern aspects and none was in pinyon–juniper patches less than 4.8 ha in size. Based on our results and other available records, we do not believe that accipiter nesting use of pinyon–juniper vegetation is restricted to northwestern Colorado. Federal lands contain and estimated 65% of current pinyon-juniper vegetation, and we recommend that federal land managers consider the potential of these areas to support nesting accipiters during land management planning. We identified the BLM and U.S. Forest Service field and district offices with the greatest pinyon–juniper coverage, and provide some general recommendations for accipiter nest surveys in this vegetation type.

# Acknowledgements

This project was undertaken with funding provided by BLM Assistance Agreement JSA065003. We thank our seasonal field technicians, James Cederstrom, Corey Kanuckel, and Robert Spaul, for their dedication to the field effort, as well as HawkWatch International staff biologist Mike Neal for his assistance in the field. We thank Ed Hollowed and Brett Smithers of the WRFO for providing raptor survey data, their insight into accipiter nesting use of pinyon–juniper in the Piceance Basin and northwestern Colorado, and reviews of this report. We thank the BLM Rawlins, Wyoming Field Office for providing additional accipiter nesting data used for comparative purposes. This technical report also benefited from input provided by the project's BLM Steering Committee, which included Dave Mills (BLM Utah, Richfield Field Office), Steve Madsen (BLM Utah State Office), Dave Roberts (BLM Wyoming State Office), and Wes Anderson (BLM Colorado State Office), as well as independent reviews by Bill Mannan (University of Arizona) and Richard Reynolds (USDA Forest Service, Rocky Mountain Research Station, CO).

Three accipiter species breed in North America, the Sharp-shinned Hawk (*Accipiter striatus*), Cooper's Hawk (*A. cooperii*), and Northern Goshawk (*A. gentilis*). Accipiters are known to use a variety of habitats for nesting throughout the United States, but in the West, attention has focused primarily on conifer-dominated habitats (Rosenfield and Bielefeldt 1993, Squires and Reynolds 1997, Bildstein and Meyer 2000). Very little published information is available on accipiter nesting use of pinyon–juniper habitats (in most of western U.S., typically *Pinus edulis* or *monophylla* – *Juniperus* spp.), although use is known outside the nesting season (e.g., Northern Goshawk use of pinyon–juniper habitats during post-fledgling dispersal and winter periods; Drennan and Beier 2003, Kennedy and Ward 2003, Wiens et al. 2006). The scarcity of information on nesting use of pinyon– juniper habitats in part may be due to a bias toward searching for nests in habitats assumed a priori to be suitable (Siders and Kennedy 1996, Squires and Reynolds 1997). It is also possible, however, that pinyon–juniper habitats do not regularly provide the individual tree, habitat, or landscape-structure characteristics sought by nesting accipiters, as pinyon–juniper woodlands are often more shrub-like and open relative to other conifer woodlands.

Nesting habitat characteristics vary for all three North American accipiters. Historically, it was believed that habitat characteristics varied in relation to accipiter body size. For example, it has been hypothesized that the smaller Sharp-shinned Hawk selects smaller trees and denser woodlands, the Cooper's Hawk medium-sized trees and medium-density woodlands, and the larger Northern Goshawk the largest trees and most open woodlands. While some studies have found support for this body-size hypothesis (Reynolds et al. 1982, Moore and Henny 1983, Trexel et al. 1999), others have found that few nesting habitat characteristics follow the predicted trends and that much variability and overlap exists for each species (Hennessy 1978, Siders and Kennedy 1994, Siders and Kennedy 1996). Not surprisingly, it does appear that overlap is most likely to occur between species closer to one another in size; i.e., Sharp-shinned Hawk and Northern Goshawk nesting habitat characteristics are most often distinct from each other (e.g., Hennessy 1978, Siders and Kennedy 1996). Additionally, the preference of Northern Goshawks for more mature forest stands is well-documented (Squires and Reynolds 1997).

Given these considerations, one might expect Northern Goshawks to be the least likely of the three accipiter

species to make use of pinyon–juniper habitats for nesting. Indeed, an extensive review of the literature revealed only a single documented case of a Northern Goshawk nesting in pinyon–juniper habitat (Johansson et al. 1994), no published reports of Cooper's Hawks nesting in pinyon–juniper, and only two studies that recorded Sharp-shinned Hawks nesting in pinyon–juniper and juniper habitats (Platt 1976, Hennessy 1978). Note that few of the studies reviewed actually searched pinyon–juniper habitats for accipiter nests, and therefore, the previously mentioned bias may partially account for the few available published records. Unpublished raptor survey records from the White River Field Office (WRFO) of the Bureau of Land Management (BLM) suggest that accipiters, especially Cooper's Hawks, may use pinyon–juniper for nesting more commonly than previously believed (Ed Hollowed and Brett Smithers, BLM-WRFO, personal communication).

Pinyon–juniper habitats are found scattered throughout the western United States and occupy and estimated 20.9 million hectares of western land (Smith et al. 2004). It is widely believed that pinyon–juniper vegetation has expanded in distribution and density over the last 150 years, driven by a complex of human-caused environmental changes (Tausch et al. 1981). In the United States, the majority (83%) of pinyon–juniper vegetation occurs in New Mexico, Arizona, Utah, Nevada, and Colorado (in order of total land area). Federal lands contain 65% of all pinyon–juniper habitats (Smith et al. 2004). The BLM manages the largest share of these lands (56%), followed by the U.S. Forest Service (USFS; 40%) and other federal agencies (4%; Pugh 2004). Pinyon–juniper habitats on public lands are subjected to various human-associated activities that may compromise potential nesting habitat. These activities include prescribed burns, mechanical treatments (i.e., chaining, plowing, disking, or related tillage treatments), chemical treatments, timber harvest, energy extraction, livestock grazing, and recreation.

If accipiter nesting use of pinyon–juniper woodlands is not an isolated phenomenon, federal land-management agencies need to be informed of this and be provided with survey guidance for the protection of accipiter nests in these habitats. All three accipiter species are protected by the Migratory Bird Treaty Act, which prohibits the "taking" of these species, their young, or nests. Additionally, the U.S. Fish and Wildlife Service (USFWS) has been petitioned to list the Northern Goshawk under the Endangered Species Act on numerous occasions and, although these petitions have been denied, the USFWS and USFS consider goshawks a species of concern, and the BLM lists it as sensitive in six states (Squires and Kennedy 2006).

The specific objectives of our research were to:

1) Assess accipiter use of pinyon–juniper habitats for nesting in the Piceance Basin of Colorado.

2) Describe basic vegetation and landscape characteristics of accipiter nest sites found in pinyon–juniper vegetation in the study area.

3) Provide federal land managers with accipiter survey recommendations relating to pinyon–juniper habitats.

## Study Area

The Piceance Basin study area was located in Rio Blanco County in northwestern Colorado, approximately 12 km west of the town of Meeker (Figure 1). The study area encompassed 2,112 km², 86% of which is managed by the BLM WRFO. The remainder is privately owned or managed by the state of Colorado. Elevations in the study area ranged from 1,671–2,554 m, and annual precipitation in Meeker averaged 42 cm from 1900–2007 (Western Regional Climate Center, Reno, NV). The study area is best characterized as a series of predominantly pinyon–juniper ridges, intermixed with small Wyoming and mountain sagebrush (*Artemisia tridentata wyomingensis* and *A. t. vaseyana*) openings, and separated by narrow, ephemeral drainages dominated by basin big sagebrush (*A. t. tridentata*). Pinyon–juniper vegetation was most common and reached its greatest stature along numerous ridges within the area. The Piceance Basin was undergoing extensive natural-gas development during the study, and gas wells, associated roads, and human activity were common in the study area. The WRFO manages a database of raptor nest locations documented within

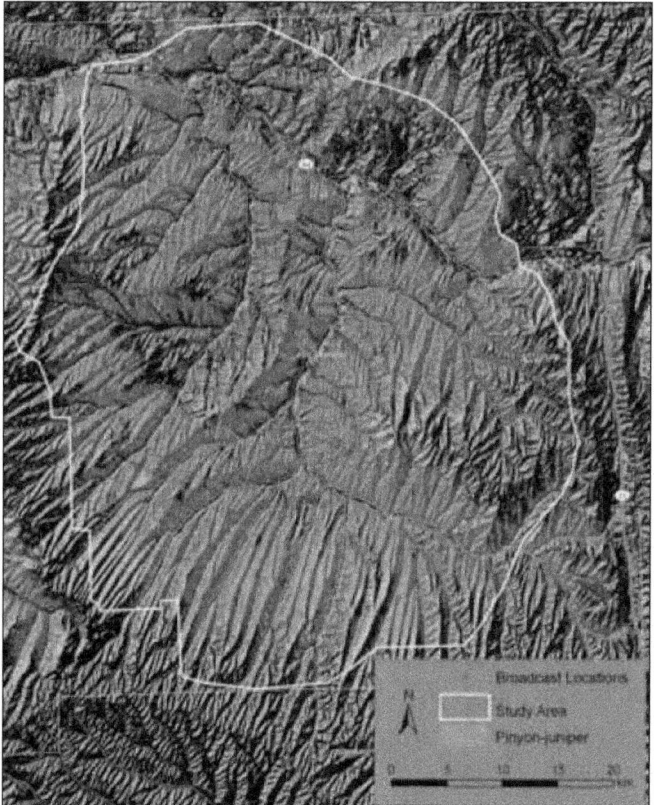

**Figure 1.** Piceance Basin study area in northwestern Colorado, with areas of pinyon–juniper vegetation and locations of 2007 broadcast surveys shown.

the field office, gathered by field-office personnel and gas-industry consultants. Between 1987 and 2003, only five active (eggs laid) accipiter nests were located in the Piceance Basin study area; however, 11 active nests were found in 2005 and six active nests were found in 2006.

## Accipiter Broadcast Surveys

To detect accipiters, we used broadcast surveys from unpaved roads transecting larger patches of pinyon–juniper within the study area. We acknowledge that constraining our surveys to roads potentially biased our effort with regard to extrapolating results to the larger landscape; however, our intent was not to develop a rigorous assessment of nesting density or overall distribution. Instead, we sought simply to confirm presence of the three species in pinyon-juniper habitats of the area and then locate sufficient numbers of active or recently used nesting territories to enable reasonable, initial quantification of the site and nest characteristics involved. Moreover, in this particular landscape, pinyon-juniper habitat is distributed primarily along relatively narrow side ridgelines interspersed with finger canyons and drainages, and most such ridges have dirt roads that lead up them from the basin below to the main ridgetop above. Therefore, the available road network comprised a nearly systematic and highly representative series of transects from which to conduct the surveys. That said, the one component of pinyon-juniper habitat that surveying only along these roads may not have sampled well is isolated patches of particularly steep, rugged, and largely inaccessible habitat located near the tops of some of the ravines. In many cases, however, we were able to survey at least partially even these habitats by virtue of broadcasting from roads that ran along the main ridgetop above. We also did not estimate the probability of detection during our surveys, which imparts an unknown bias with respect to using our survey results to estimate overall abundances and nesting densities across the broader landscape.

Previous research suggested that accipiter broadcast surveys may be most effective during courtship and nestling periods (Rosenfield et al. 1988, Kennedy and Stahlecker 1993, Joy et al. 1994); however, surveys during the post-fledging period also may be effective due to the increased number of potential responders (i.e., adults plus young; R. Reynolds, personal communication). To increase our chances of detecting all three accipiter species, which generally vary in their nesting chronology, we conducted two rounds of surveys between 30 April and 1 June and between 4 June and 7 July. We based our broadcast survey methods on those outlined by Rosenfield et al. (1988) and Kennedy and Stahlecker (1993), with modifications to suit our specific needs. We established broadcast stations every 300 m along sections of accessible road traversing pinyon–juniper habitat, with the first station in a particular patch established 150 m from the patch edge. We based our choice of spacing between stations on evaluating literature concerning typical spacing of accipiter nesting areas and rough estimates of the broadcast range of our caller, striving for an interval we felt would maximize our chances of detecting any existing territories. We also limited our surveys to road sections that transected (or in very few cases paralleled along one side of and immediately adjacent to) a minimum of 200 m of continuous pinyon-juniper habitat, again based on review of the literature concerning typical minimum forest-patch sizes occupied by nesting accipiters. Surveyors used portable GPS units (Garmin GPSMAP 60CSx) to record all survey routes and station points.

At each station, the observer broadcast alarm calls in four directions, at 45° angles to the road. Surveyors reduced the number of broadcast directions to two if a patch was located on only one side of the road. Each 10-sec broadcast in a specific direction was followed by 30 sec of scanning and listening for responses. At each station, the observer broadcast Sharp-shinned Hawk, Cooper's Hawk, and Northern Goshawk alarm calls, in that order, to avoid potential size-related inhibitory effects. When a focal species was detected, the observer recorded the species, age, and sex, when possible; an assessment of the observer's confidence in identifying the responding species (i.e., confident or not confident, as supported by a description of what was heard and/or seen); time of response; time elapsed since first call broadcast; species of call broadcasted immediately preceding the detection; response type (i.e., call, call and approach, call and fly-by, silent approach, silent fly-by); estimated distance and bearing to response; station number and location; and general vegetation characteristics surrounding the detection point (i.e., maturity and stature of pinyon–juniper vegetation). Appendix A contains an example of the data sheet used during the broadcast surveys.

While time of day may or may not influence response rates of accipiters to broadcast calls (e.g., see Kimmel and Yahner [1990] and Roberson et al. [2005] for differing perspectives), lighting undoubtedly affects an observer's ability to visually detect non-vocal responses. To reduce variation in conditions affecting response detection, all surveys occurred between 30 min after sunrise and 30 min before sunset, and only during periods of fair weather

(i.e., no rain, snow, or winds exceeding 20 kph) and no heavy vehicle passage. The volume of all broadcast calls was approximately 110 dB at 1 m from the source (Fuller and Mosher 1987), which we achieved by connecting a portable MP3 player to a hand-held megaphone.

## Nest Searches

We used broadcast-survey detection locations to guide on-foot nest searches later in July (to correspond to likely post-hatch periods and reduce the likelihood of nest desertion). To augment nest sample sizes, we also attempted to revisit nests found between 2005 and 2007 by BLM and industry personnel. As noted in the study area description, only a few, scattered accipiter nest records were available from before this period. "Active" nests were identified as those for which we obtained positive confirmation of incubation, adult behavior indicative of nestling attendance (e.g., feeding, mantling, etc.), fresh prey remains or extensive whitewash indicative of extended nestling presence, or actual eggs or nestlings.

## Vegetation and GIS-based Metrics

We collected detailed vegetation data around identified, active accipiter nests after young had fledged (i.e., during mid- and late July). Vegetation sampling followed methods developed by James and Shugart (1970) and Noon (1981), with minor modifications to suit our specific needs. Sampling occurred within 0.04-ha circular plots centered on nests, with each plot divided into quadrats by two perpendicular, 11.3-m long, crossed transects aligned with the cardinal directions. Within each quadrant, the number of live and dead trees in 10 diameter-at-breast-height (DBH) size classes was recorded: <3, 3–8, 8–15, 15–23, 23–38, 38–53, 53–69, 69–84, 84–102, and >102 cm (James and Shugart 1970). Surveyors also recorded the number of fallen logs ≥1.5 m long and ≥8 cm diameter in each quadrant (Noon 1981). Surveyors estimated shrub density by walking the perpendicular transects and counting the number of live and dead shrubs occurring within the span of the observer's outstretched arms. We multiplied the number of shrubs encountered within a subplot by 125 to produce an estimate of shrub density per hectare (Noon 1981). Surveyors estimated canopy and ground cover by walking the two transects, stopping on each alternate step, and sighting up and down through an ocular tube with crossed sights. Thus, they recorded the number of canopy and ground vegetation "hits" at 20 stops (James and Shugart 1970). Nest-specific measures included the nest-tree species, overall height, lower canopy height, and DBH;

the height of the nest above the ground; and the nest dimensions. Total-plot (i.e., nest site) measures included species-specific tree densities and average DBHs; density of species-specific saplings (i.e., trees <3 cm DBH); density of downed logs ≥1.5 m long; percent canopy and ground cover; and shrub density. Appendix A contains an example of the vegetation data sheet used.

We used a GIS incorporating a 30-m resolution digital elevation model (DEM) and 1-m resolution aerial photography (captured in 2006) to provide additional insight into nest-site and overall patch characteristics at active nests. From the DEM, we determined the elevation, slope, and aspect of each nest site. From the aerial photos, we determined the distance from each nest site to the nearest habitat edge (i.e., a discernable road, pipeline or other gas and oil infrastructure, powerline right-of-way, or sagebrush or grass opening) and the minimum width of the patch associated with each nest site. We assessed the latter by identifying and measuring the shortest axes through the nest-site habitat patches to the nearest two patch breaks, with relevant breaks defined as those corresponding to adjacent habitat patches of at least 30 m by 30 m in size (i.e., excluding small roads or other narrow linear features). We used all known 2005–2007 active nests to provide initial, rough (due to possible survey biases) estimates of average nearest-neighbor distances for each species, with the distances calculated for each nest on an annual basis and averaged across years.

Due to small sample sizes for each accipiter species, we limited our analysis to species-by-species univariate $t$-tests (alpha = 0.05, separate variances assumed). We also present a full complement of descriptive statistics for each metric to provide land managers with a basic sketch of potential accipiter nesting habitat.

Because our nest samples cannot be considered either exhaustive or completely random, we caution that the results of our habitat and inter-specific analyses should be considered preliminary indicators that may be confounded by unknown sampling biases. For example, the characteristics we describe may be more representative of birds nesting near roads than the population as whole. In this particular case, however, with regard to the primary motivation behind our research—expanding knowledge of nesting accipiters in a habitat that is broadly subject to oil and gas development—this bias may in fact be entirely appropriate given the close relationship between roads and development activities.

We detected probable accipiter responses during 66 of 541 (12%) broadcast surveys conducted during the 2007 nesting season. After consolidating proximate (i.e., <1 km apart) responses from the same species (either within or between survey periods) and removing responses with low observer confidence, we produced distinct, confident response locations for 2 Sharp-shinned Hawks, 22 Cooper's Hawks, and 4 Northern Goshawks. We documented responses during both survey rounds at 7 Cooper's Hawk and 1 Northern Goshawk response locations.

Our 2007 surveyors found no active Sharp-shinned Hawk nests, 13 active Cooper's Hawk nests, and 3 active Northern Goshawk nests. They found seven of the active Cooper's Hawk nests and one of the active Northern Goshawk nests during nest searches conducted from broadcast response locations. Other active nests were located by BLM personnel, industry consultants, and incidentally by our surveyors. We illustrate examples of typical nesting situations for each species in Appendix B. Vegetation surveys occurred at 3 Sharp-shinned Hawk, 10 Cooper's Hawk, and 10 Northern Goshawk nests. We used nests located in 2005 and 2006 to augment vegetation survey locations for all three species. We did not conduct vegetation surveys at four Cooper's Hawk nests discovered in 2007 to avoid disturbance of nests with young still in them. We were unable to obtain a larger sample of Sharp-shinned Hawk nests due to difficulty relocating nests from previous years and an inability to assign a confident species association to located nests. We included in our vegetation surveys only nests with confirmed species associations, based on documented activity or nest size.

Vegetation data and GIS-metrics suggested that nest-site characteristics of Sharp-shinned Hawks, Cooper's Hawks, and Northern Goshawks commonly overlapped (Table 1). Nests of all three species were located in both pinyon and juniper trees, but most Northern Goshawk nests (90%) were in pinyon pines. Although limited by small sample sizes, our results suggest that Sharp-shinned Hawk nest sites contained significantly smaller DBH pinyon pines, smaller DBH live trees, and a greater density of 15–23 cm DBH trees than those of the other two species (Table 1). In addition, Sharp-shinned Hawks nests were

lower in the nest tree relative to Cooper's Hawk nests, and their nest sites contained a greater density of live trees and 8–15 cm DBH trees compared to Northern Goshawks. Cooper's Hawk and Northern Goshawk nest and nest-site characteristics only differed in regards to distance to edge, with Northern Goshawk nests found closer to edges. All three species used nest sites with very similar average canopy cover (64–65%) and densities of live trees between 23–38 cm DBH (168–175 trees/ha). All surveyed accipiter nests were on aspects between 205° and 81° (Figure 2). Average elevations and slopes at nest sites were similar for all three species, whereas average distance to road and edge were lower at Northern Goshawk nest sites (Table 1). The shortest minimum patch axis of all three species was very similar and had a lower bound of 221–229 m. This equates to a minimum pinyon–juniper patch size of 4.8–5.2 ha surrounding surveyed accipiter nests. Average nearest-neighbor nesting distance was 9.0 ± SE of 3.3 km for Sharp-shinned Hawks ($n = 5$ [note: $n$ is the number of distances calculated between active nests, not the total number of nests]), 6.0 ± 1.1 km for Cooper's Hawks ($n = 19$), and 10.2 ± 1.8 km for Northern Goshawks ($n = 3$). During the 2007 nesting season, a minimum of 13

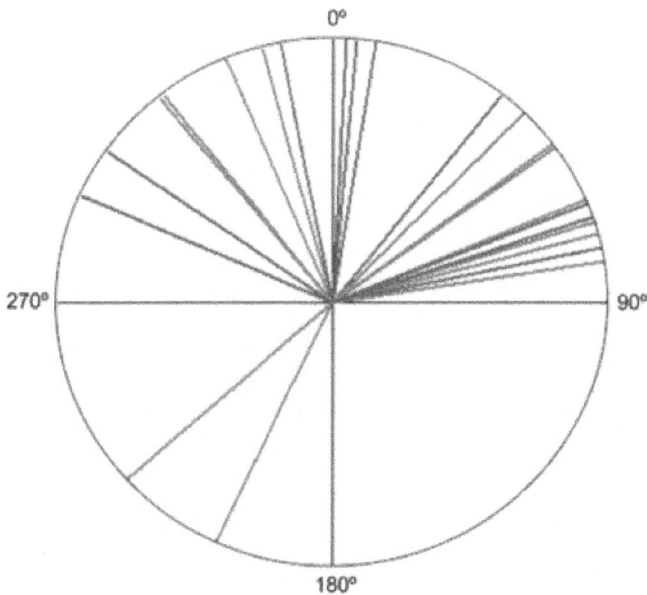

**Figure 2.** Aspect of Sharp-shinned Hawk (red; $n = 3$), Cooper's Hawk (blue; $n = 10$), and Northern Goshawk (green; $n = 10$) nest sites in the Piceance Basin study area.

**Table 1.** Vegetation and GIS-based metrics at Sharp-shinned Hawk (*n* = 3), Coopers' Hawk (*n* = 10), and Northern Goshawk (*n* = 10) nests in pinyon–juniper habitats of the Piceance Basin, Colorado study area.

| Vegetation or GIS metric | Sharp-shinned Hawk Mean (SE)[1] | Range | Cooper's Hawk Mean (SE) | Range | Northern Goshawk Mean (SE) | Range |
|---|---|---|---|---|---|---|
| Nest tree DBH (cm) | 32 (8) | 19–46 | 45 (6) | 31–93 | 43 (5) | 31–77 |
| Nest height (m) | 16 (1)$^A$ | 15–18 | 22 (2)$^B$ | 17–32 | 18 (1)$^{AB}$ | 12–26 |
| Tree height (m) | 23 (2) | 21–26 | 27 (2) | 20–40 | 26 (1) | 20–34 |
| Lower canopy height (m) | 6 (1) | 4–7 | 6 (1) | 3–9 | 4 (0) | 3–6 |
| Ground cover (%) | 5 (0) | 5–5 | 23 (4) | 5–40 | 21 (3) | 5–40 |
| Canopy cover (%) | 65 (8) | 55–80 | 64 (4) | 45–85 | 65 (3) | 55–90 |
| Live shrubs per ha | 45 (22) | 5–80 | 100 (23) | 10–245 | 74 (24) | 25–265 |
| Dead shrubs per ha | 12 (12) | 0–35 | 7 (3) | 0–20 | 4 (2) | 0–15 |
| Avg. pinyon DBH (cm) | 17 (3)$^A$ | 14–23 | 36 (3)$^B$ | 19–53 | 29 (2)$^B$ | 21–41 |
| Avg. juniper DBH (cm) | 28 (3) | 23–34 | 29 (3) | 18–44 | 31 (3) | 18–44 |
| Avg. live tree DBH (cm) | 21 (2)$^A$ | 17–25 | 30 (3)$^B$ | 16–43 | 29 (2)$^B$ | 19–42 |
| Avg. dead tree DBH (cm) | 17 (4) | 11–25 | 22 (5) | 10–61 | 20 (5) | 12–61 |
| Pinyons per ha | 450 (95) | 275–600 | 345 (102) | 75–1175 | 278 (33) | 100–450 |
| Junipers per ha | 300 (38) | 250–375 | 198 (30) | 100–400 | 245 (34) | 75–425 |
| Live trees per ha | 750 (58)$^A$ | 650–850 | 543 (100)$^A$ | 275–1375 | 523 (47)$^B$ | 275–725 |
| Dead trees per ha | 133 (8) | 125–150 | 133 (25) | 25–275 | 115 (34) | 25–325 |
| Saplings per ha | 267 (169) | 50–600 | 315 (94) | 0–900 | 430 (72) | 0–725 |
| Downed logs per ha | 283 (17) | 250–300 | 458 (80) | 125–900 | 318 (66) | 0–650 |
| 3–8 cm DBH trees per ha | 100 (52) | 0–175 | 70 (40) | 0–400 | 50 (16) | 0s125 |
| 8–15 cm DBH trees per ha | 167 (46)$^A$ | 75–225 | 108 (50)$^A$ | 25–550 | 73 (18)$^B$ | 0–150 |
| 15–23 cm DBH trees per ha | 242 (22)$^A$ | 200–275 | 73 (21)$^B$ | 0–200 | 88 (21)$^B$ | 0–200 |
| 23–38 cm DBH trees per ha | 175 (29) | 125–225 | 175 (38) | 0–350 | 168 (27) | 25–300 |
| 38–53 cm DBH trees per ha | 58 (17) | 25–75 | 83 (14) | 25–150 | 108 (24) | 25–250 |
| 53–61 cm DBH trees per ha | 0 (0) | 0 | 25 (10) | 0–100 | 23 (9) | 0–75 |
| 61–84 cm DBH trees per ha | 8 (8) | 0–25 | 5 (3) | 0–25 | 15 (8) | 0–75 |
| 84–102 cm DBH trees per ha | 0 (0) | 0 | 3 (3) | 0–25 | 0 (0) | 0 |
| >102 cm DBH trees per ha | 0 (0) | 0 | 3 (3) | 0–25 | 0 (0) | 0 |
| Aspect (30-m cell) | – | 228–68 | – | 294–78 | – | 205–81 |
| Elevation (30-m cell) | 2061 (63) | 1996–2187 | 2039 (21) | 1896–2108 | 2075 (20) | 1970–2144 |
| Degree slope (30-m cell) | 10 (2) | 8–13 | 7 (1) | 2–11 | 7 (1) | 2–14 |
| Distance to road (m) | 212 (64) | 85–285 | 222 (59) | 74–611 | 131 (37) | 34–425 |
| Distance to edge (m) | 130 (80)$^{AB}$ | 21–285 | 146 (23)$^A$ | 56–283 | 78 (16)$^B$ | 34–196 |
| Shortest patch axis (m) | 658 (224) | 227–978 | 523 (78) | 229–980 | 627 (109) | 221–1048 |

[1] Where significant differences among means for different species occurred, within rows means that do not share superscript letters indicate significant differences (univariate *t*-test, $P \leq 0.05$).

Cooper's Hawk and 3 Northern Goshawk nests were active in the Piceance Basin study area. Additional consideration of confident broadcast responses in conjunction with active nest locations suggested possible totals of 2 Sharp-shinned Hawk, 29 Cooper's Hawk, and 6 Northern Goshawk nests in surveyed areas. The WRFO raptor database contained records of five active Sharp-shinned Hawk and seven active Cooper's Hawk nests in 2005, and two active nests of each of the three accipiter species in 2006. It is important to note that these nests were located through clearance surveys in association with proposed gas development, and therefore were not intended to provide a comprehensive inventory of the area. As a result, even taken all together, these figures probably under-represent the potential total number of accipiter nests active each year in pinyon-juniper habitat within the Piceance Basin. Because we did not quantify the probability of detection for our surveys, and therefore cannot confidently establish accurate estimates of spatial representation, we cannot provide more confident assessments of overall abundance or density by extrapolating across the broader landscape.

Our results clearly demonstrate that all three accipiter species will utilize pinyon-juniper for nesting, with the Cooper's Hawk apparently the most likely to do so. Our work suggests, however, that the density of nesting accipiters in pinyon-juniper is likely low compared to other North American vegetation types. Average nest spacing of accipiters reported by other studies ranges from 1.2–5.6 km (Rosenfield and Bielefeldt 1993, Squires and Reynolds 1997, Bildstein and Meyer 2000, Reynolds, et al. 2005). Due to limitations of our survey effort, we cannot confidently claim to have generated truly representative samples and, if anything, our samples likely under-represent the overall abundance of nesting accipiters in the pinyon-juniper habitats sampled. This may be particularly true for Northern Goshawks, which other research has shown may require 3–4 broadcast surveys per season to yield robust assessments of presence/absence (Boyce et al. 2005). Nevertheless, based on what we did document, only the Cooper's Hawk even approached the upper range of previously documented nearest-neighbor distances, averaging 6.0 km between nests.

Similar to results previously reported in studies conducted in other western conifer habitats (Siders and Kennedy 1994, Siders and Kennedy 1996), we found considerable overlap between the nest-site characteristics of the three species. Although compromised by small samples sizes

and possibly non-random sampling, our results suggest, however, that Sharp-shinned Hawks used nest sites featuring primarily smaller trees and a greater overall density of small trees compared to their larger congeners. This result appears to agree with accipiter body-size predictions of nesting habitat use; i.e., that the smaller Sharp-shinned Hawk will utilize young, dense patches containing smaller trees relative to the larger accipiters. In contrast, the Cooper's Hawk and Northern Goshawk overlapped in most nest-tree and nest-site characteristics. Reciprocal use of nests has been documented for these two species on the Kaibab Plateau (R. Reynolds, personal communication) and may have contributed to the overlap in nest site characteristics if this phenomenon is also occurring in the Piceance Basin. Compared to the Sharp-shinned Hawk, both Cooper's Hawks and Northern Goshawks apparently used nest sites with larger diameter trees and lower densities of small trees. In addition, Northern Goshawk nest sites contained a lower density of all trees relative to the Sharp-shinned Hawk, likely reflecting their preference from more mature, open forest stands (Squires and Reynolds 1997). Overall, the characteristics of accipiter nest sites in pinyon-juniper woodlands appear to fall within the range of variation of basic nest-site characteristics (e.g., nest tree height and DBH, and average site tree DBH and density) recorded in other western forests (e.g., Reynolds et al. 1982, Siders and Kennedy 1994, Siders and Kennedy 1996). We found accipiter nests most commonly on slopes with northwestern through eastern aspects, and none on southeastern exposures (Figure 2). Other western accipiter studies have reported similar results (Hennessy 1978, Reynolds et al. 1978, Moore and Henny 1983, Kennedy 1988). Our results also suggested a minimum patch size of 4.8-ha for accipiters nesting within pinyon-juniper patches, which is similar to the finding that Northern Goshawks nesting in California occupied only stands >4.1 ha in size (Woodbridge and Detrich 1994).

Although we did not detect a high density of nesting accipiters in the Piceance Basin study area, we do not believe their use of pinyon-juniper for nesting is unique to northwestern Colorado. Few published studies have documented accipiter nesting use of these habitats, but this may be due to nest-search biases (Siders and Kennedy 1996, Squires and Reynolds 1997). That said, the only previously published account of Northern Goshawk nesting use of pinyon-juniper indicated that a fairly high 13% ($n$ = 30) of known nests were located in this vegetation type (Johansson et al. 1994). Platt (1976) reported that 44% ($n$ = 61) of Sharp-shinned Hawk nests examined in Utah were located in conifer trees, including pinyon and juniper, but the author did not provide any additional detail. In the Wasatch–Cache National Forest of northeastern Utah, 20% ($n = 20$) of Sharp-shinned Hawk nests were found in juniper (Hennessy 1978). While this is the extent of the formally published record, additional records do exist. For example, Smith and Hutchins (2006, 2007) opportunistically documented two Cooper's Hawk nests in junipers and a third in a pinyon pine in northeastern Nevada and northwestern Utah. Similarly, although not located in pinyon–juniper habitat, five Cooper's Hawk nests in south-central Wyoming were located in juniper trees (H. Cline, BLM Rawlins Field Office, personal communication). It is quite likely that additional unpublished records exist in databases maintained by various state and federal agencies.

# Recommendations for Pinyon–Juniper Accipiter Nest Surveys

The previous discussion suggests that accipiters nesting in pinyon–juniper habitats is not a phenomenon restricted to northwestern Colorado. With federal agencies managing 65% of all pinyon–juniper habitats (Smith et al. 2004), it is critical that they are aware of the heretofore largely overlooked potential of these habitats to support nesting accipiters. We recommend that federal agencies responsible for managing pinyon–juniper habitats make an effort to incorporate this knowledge during land-use planning, and conduct surveys for nesting accipiters when management actions that may affect pinyon–juniper habitats are proposed (i.e., prescribed burns, mechanical/chemical treatments, timber harvest, energy extraction, etc.). We have identified BLM field offices and USFS district offices with substantial coverage (>50,000 ha) of pinyon–juniper woodlands on public lands (Table 2).

**Table 2.** Bureau of Land Management (BLM) and U.S. Forest Service (USFS) field and district offices with greater than 50,000 ha of pinyon–juniper (P–J) habitat on public lands, ranked by total coverage area (compiled from Pugh [2004]).

| BLM Field Office | States | P–J cover (1,000s of ha) | USFS District Office | States | P–J cover (1,000s of ha) |
|---|---|---|---|---|---|
| Ely | NV | 1313 | Humboldt-Toiyabe | NV, CA | 973 |
| Battle Mountain | NV | 527 | Gila | NM | 599 |
| Grand Staircase-Escalante NM FO | UT | 399 | Cibola | NM | 312 |
| | | | Tonto | AZ | 301 |
| Cedar City | UT | 383 | Kaibab | AZ | 286 |
| Arizona Strip | AZ | 324 | Apache-Sitgreaves | AZ | 280 |
| Elko | NV | 299 | Lincoln | NM | 249 |
| Monticello | UT | 297 | Coconino | AZ | 249 |
| Price | UT | 267 | Dixie | UT | 217 |
| White River | CO | 267 | Prescott | AZ | 207 |
| Richfield | UT | 230 | Modoc | CA | 202 |
| Grand Junction | CO | 226 | Fishlake | UT | 179 |
| Carson City | NV | 221 | Santa Fe | NM | 179 |
| Moab | UT | 220 | Carson | NM | 145 |
| Dolores | CO | 211 | Coronado | AZ, NM | 119 |
| Farmington | NM | 174 | Inyo | CA | 108 |
| Uncompahgre | CO | 173 | Manti-LaSal | UT | 102 |
| Vernal | UT | 172 | Grand Mesa-Uncomp-Gunnison | CO | 66 |
| Fillmore | UT | 159 | Ochoco | OR | 62 |
| Royal Gorge | CO | 140 | Los Padres | CA | 56 |
| Salt Lake | UT | 137 | San Juan | CO | 50 |
| Little Snake | CO | 117 | | | |
| Kanab | UT | 116 | | | |
| Rio Puerco | NM | 107 | | | |
| Deschutes | OR | 103 | | | |
| Glenwood Springs | CO | 94 | | | |
| Alturas | CA | 90 | | | |
| Saint George | UT | 77 | | | |
| Winnemucca | NV | 75 | | | |
| Taos | NM | 73 | | | |
| Kingman | AZ | 66 | | | |
| Soccoro | NM | 59 | | | |
| Three Rivers | OR | 53 | | | |
| Owyhee | ID | 53 | | | |
| Rock Springs | WY | 52 | | | |

Managers of these federal lands should be particularly cognizant of the potential for accipiters to nest in pinyon–juniper habitats.

Numerous documents outlining raptor nest-survey protocols exist; hence, we do not provide a detailed overview of survey methodologies here. Instead, it is our intention to provide guidance in the identification of potential pinyon–juniper habitats for survey, suggest specific survey techniques based on our experiences during this study, and highlight attributes of accipiter nesting ecology that may aid nest surveyors.

Pinyon–juniper woodlands are highly variable in terms of relative pinyon and juniper composition, tree age and stature, and associated vegetation composition (i.e., pinyon–juniper does not represent a single natural land type; Tausch 1999). As a result, the value of pinyon–juniper to nesting accipiters likely varies widely across the West and among local landscapes. To assess fully the potential value of pinyon–juniper habitats to accipiters at a specific locale will require the identification of patches meeting the nest-site characteristics sought by these species. Although Table 1 and example photographs of typical nest-site vegetation provided in Appendix B provide some initial insight into these characteristics, our results are based on limited sample sizes, and additional work is needed to refine further our understanding of accipiter nesting use of this vegetation type. Additionally, we recognize that obtaining a detailed characterization of pinyon–juniper habitats is often prohibitive. Therefore, we recommend that land managers initially use coarse-scale approaches to identify potential pinyon–juniper accipiter nesting habitat.

We suggest that land managers begin with the identification of pinyon–juniper habitats on their lands, then isolate patches meeting minimum patch-size requirements for nesting accipiters (i.e., ≥4.8 ha), and finally focus in on patches likely to contain higher densities of 23–38 cm DBH trees. Again, we stress that further refinement of an accipiter nest-site "search image" will require additional research in this vegetation type, and it is possible that accipiters will be found nesting in a wider range of conditions in different localities (e.g., smaller patches or wider range of canopy covers). Vegetation maps depicting the distribution of pinyon–juniper habitats are available through a variety of sources (e.g., see Smith et al. 2004, USGS National Gap Analysis Program 2004) and many federal land managers possess their own highly detailed vegetation maps. High-resolution (1 m) aerial photography is available for much of the United States from the U.S. Department of Agriculture (http://datagateway.nrcs.usda.

gov/). Aerial photography can be used to refine existing vegetation maps, as well as to assess patch size and tree density. Identification of patches with larger trees can be accomplished by using GIS software combined with field-personnel knowledge of where such patches occur. While some research suggests that there is no strong association between pinyon–juniper woodlands and any particular aspect (Tausch et al. 1981), in some areas, larger trees appear to occur on north facing slopes due to the relatively moist and cool conditions found there (Lei 1999). Although the establishment and stature of pinyon–juniper woodlands are influenced by topography, soil, elevation, latitude, disturbance, and other environmental conditions in complex ways (Tausch 1999), we believe it should be possible to identify where pinyon–juniper patches containing larger trees are most likely to occur in a given area with the aid of GIS software, DEMs (from which elevation, slope, and aspect can be derived), aerial photography, and limited ground-truthing.

If broadcast surveys are used to locate nests, we suggest playing Sharp-shinned Hawk calls first and Northern Goshawk calls last, to avoid potential interspecific inhibitory effects. Alternatively, broadcasting Great Horned Owl calls also is effective in eliciting responses from a variety of raptor species (Mosher and Fuller 1996). Personnel conducting broadcast surveys should be aware that jays often mimic broadcasts. For example, Steller's jays (*Cyanocitta stelleri*) accounted for 17% of all "positive" broadcast survey detections in New Mexico (Kennedy and Stahlecker 1993). When they detect a response, we suggest that personnel record their confidence level in the assessment of the responding species and provide detailed notes based on that confidence level. Additionally, we recommend surveyors employ a minimum of two broadcast survey rounds during the nesting season, but as many as three or four intensive surveys may be required to accurately assess their presence/absence or generate robust estimates of goshawk abundance (Boyce et al. 2005). More generally, if the goal is to generate accurate assessments of nesting density or more thoroughly evaluate presence/absence of nesting birds in a specific area, more extensive, systematic surveys than we did in this study, as well as rigorous assessments of the probability of detection in the particular habitat(s) and study area of interest, will be required.

We caution that it can be very difficult to locate active accipiter nests in pinyon–juniper habitats from response locations after the birds have left the nest. We recorded responses associated with active nests as much as 540 m from the actual nest. Additionally, accipiters will often fly toward broadcast locations prior to responding.

Therefore, when attempting to locate actual nests, it is critical to visit potential vegetation during the breeding season (i.e., pair formation through post-fledging period). Although one can effectively locate nests using comprehensive foot surveys outside the breeding season, such efforts will require follow-up breeding season visits to determine nest status and species associations. Territories of all three accipiter species may contain alternate nests and individual nests may not be used in consecutive years. Northern Goshawks are the most likely to reuse nests, while Sharp-shinned Hawks and Coopers' Hawks may build a new nest each year, but often close (~100 m) to the previous year's nest (Reynolds and Wight 1978). When attempting to locate nests in pinyon–juniper, prior experience (Ed Hollowed, BLM WRFO, personal observation) and our efforts suggested that searching for stick piles on the ground (i.e., fallen nesting material; see Figure 3) was often more effective than searching within potential nest trees, as nests were often hidden by canopy vegetation.

In conclusion, we reiterate that it was not our intent here to outline thoroughly a robust survey protocol for nesting accipiters, the details of which should be designed around specific objectives and in relation to the particular habitats and study area being investigated. Other resources currently available to help guide such endeavors include, for example, U.S. Forest Service protocols for goshawk surveys (Woodbridge and Hargis 2006), a basic woodland raptor "clearance" survey protocol developed by the BLM White River Field Office (Smithers 2007), general guidelines for developing raptor nest-monitoring programs recently compiled for the BLM by Smith et al. (2009), and more generally several chapters contained in Bird and Bildstein (2007).

**Figure 3.** Typical stick pile observed below an accipiter nest in the Piceance Basin study area.

Bildstein, K. L., and K. Meyer. 2000. Sharp-shinned Hawk (*Accipiter striatus*). No. 482 *in* A. Poole and F. Gill (Editors), The birds of North America. The Birds of North America, Inc., Philadelphia, PA U.S.A.

Bird, D. M, and K. L. Bildstein (Editors). 2007. Raptor research and management techniques. Hancock House Publishers, Surrey, British Columbia, Canada, and Blaine, WA U.S.A.

Boyce, D. A., Jr., P. L. Kennedy, P. Beier, M. F. Ingraldi, S. R. MacVean, J. R. Squires, and B. Woodbridge. 2005. When are goshawks not there? Is a single visit enough to infer absence at occupied nest areas? Journal of Raptor Research 39:296–302.

Drennan, J. E., and P. Beier. 2003. Forest structure and prey abundance in winter habitat of Northern Goshawks. Journal of Wildlife Management 67:177–185.

Fuller, M. R., and J. A. Mosher. 1987. Raptor survey techniques. Pages 37–65 *in* B. A. Giron Pendleton, B. A. Millsap, K. W. Cline, and D. M. Bird (Editors), Raptor management techniques manual. National Wildlife Federation, Washington, DC, U.S.A.

Hennessy, S. P. 1978. Ecological relationships of accipiters in northern Utah–with special emphasis on the effects of human disturbance. M.S. thesis. Utah State University, Logan, UT U.S.A.

James, E. C., and H. H. Shugart, Jr. 1970. A quantitative method of habitat description. Audubon Field Notes 24:727–736.

Johansson, C., P. J. Hardin, and C. M. White. 1994. Large-area goshawk habitat modeling in Dixie National Forest using vegetation and elevation data. Studies in Avian Biology 16:50–57.

Joy, S. M., R. T. Reynolds, and D. G. Leslie. 1994. Northern Goshawk broadcast surveys: hawk response variables and survey costs. Studies in Avian Biology 16:24–30.

Kennedy, P. L. 1988. Habitat characteristics of Cooper's Hawks and Northern Goshawks nesting in New Mexico. Pages 218–227 *in* R. L. Glinski, B. G. Pendleton, M. B. Moss, M. N. LaFranc, Jr., B. A. Millsap, and S. W. Hoffman (Editors), Proceedings of the southwest raptor management symposium and workshop. National Wildlife Federation, Washington, DC, U.S.A.

Kennedy, P. L., and D. W. Stahlecker. 1993. Responsiveness of nesting Northern Goshawks to taped broadcasts of 3 conspecific calls. Journal of Wildlife Management 57:249–257.

Kennedy, P. L., and J. M. Ward. 2003. Effects of experimental food supplementation on movements of juvenile Northern Goshawks (*Accipiter gentilis atricapillus*). Oecologia 134:284–291.

Kimmel, J. T., and R. H. Yahner. 1990. Response of Northern Goshawks to taped conspecific and Great Horned Owl calls. Journal of Raptor Research 24:107–112.

Lei, S. A. 1999. Tree size and ring width of three conifers in southern Nevada. Pages 94–98 *in* S. B. Monsen and R. Stevens (Compilers), Proceedings: ecology and management of pinyon–juniper communities within the interior West. Proceedings RMRS-P-9. USDA Forest Service, Rocky Mountain Research Station, Ogden, UT U.S.A.

Moore, K. R., and C. J. Henny. 1983. Nest site characteristics of three coexisting accipiter hawks in northeastern Oregon. Journal of Raptor Research 17:65–76.

Mosher, J. A., and M. R. Fuller. 1996. Surveying woodland hawks with broadcasts of Great Horned Owl vocalizations. Wildlife Society Bulletin 24:531–536.

Noon, B. R. 1981. Techniques for sampling avian habitats. Pages 42–52 *in* D. E. Capen (Editor). The use of multivariate statistics in studies of wildlife habitat. General Technical Report RM-87. USDA Forest Service, Rocky Mountain Research Station, Fort Collins, CO U.S.A.

Platt, J. B. 1976. Sharp-shinned Hawk nesting and nest-site selection in Utah. Condor 78:102–103.

Pugh, S. A. 2004. RPA data wiz. Version 1.0. USDA Forest Service, North Central Research Station, St. Paul, MN U.S.A.

Reynolds, R. T., and H. M. Wight. 1978. Distribution, density, and productivity of accipiter hawks breeding in Oregon. Wilson Bulletin 90:182–196.

Reynolds, R. T., E. C. Meslow, and H. M. Wight. 1982. Nesting habitat of coexisting accipiter in Oregon. Journal of Wildlife Management 46:124–138.

Reynolds, R. T., J. D. Wiens, S. M. Joy, and S. R. Salafsky. 2005. Sampling considerations for demographic and habitat studies of Northern Goshawks. Journal of Raptor Research 39:274–285.

Roberson, A. M., D. E., Andersen, and P. L. Kennedy. 2005. Do breeding phase and detection distance influence the effective area surveyed for Northern Goshawks? Journal of Wildlife Management 69:1240–1250.

Rosenfield, R. N., J. Bielefeldt, and R. K. Anderson. 1988. Effectiveness of broadcast calls for detecting breeding Cooper's Hawks. Wildlife Society Bulletin 16:210–212.

Rosenfield, R. N., and J. Bielefeldt. 1993. Cooper's Hawk (*Accipiter cooperii*). No. 75 *in* A. Poole and F. Gill (Editors), The birds of North America. The Academy of Natural Sciences, Philadelphia, PA, U.S.A., and The American Ornithologists' Union, Washington, DC, U.S.A.

Siders, M. S., and P. L. Kennedy. 1994. Nesting habitat of accipiter hawks: is body size a consistent predictor of nest habitat characteristics? Studies in Avian Biology 16:92–96.

Siders, M. S., and P. L. Kennedy. 1996. Forest structural characteristics of accipiter nesting habitat: is there an allometric relationship? Condor 98:123–132.

Smith, J. P., and A. Hutchins. 2006. Northeast Nevada raptor nest survey 2005. HawkWatch International, Inc., Salt Lake City, UT U.S.A.

Smith, J. P., and A. Hutchins. 2007. Northwest Utah raptor nest survey 2006. HawkWatch International, Inc., Salt Lake City, UT U.S.A.

Smith, J. P., S. J. Slater, and M. C. Neal. 2010. Recommendations for improved raptor nest monitoring in association with oil and gas development activities. Technical Note No. 436. USDI Bureau of Land Management, Utah State Office, Salt Lake City, UT, Wyoming State Office, Cheyenne, WY, and Colorado State Office, Lakewood, CO U.S.A.

Smith, W. B., P. D. Miles, J. S. Vissage, and S. A. Pugh. 2004. Forest resources of the United States, 2002. General Technical Report NC-241. USDA Forest Service, North Central Research Station, St. Paul, MN U.S.A.

Smithers, B. 2007. BLM WRFO woodland raptor survey protocol (09-18-07). USDI Bureau of Land Management, White River Field Office, Meeker, CO U.S.A.

Squires, J. R., and P. L. Kennedy. 2006. Northern Goshawk ecology: an assessment of current knowledge and information needs for conservation and management. Studies in Avian Biology 31:63–74.

Squires, J. R., and R. T. Reynolds. 1997. Northern Goshawk (*Accipiter gentilis*). No. 298 *in* A. Poole and F. Gill (Editors), The birds of North America. The Academy of Natural Sciences, Philadelphia, PA U.S.A., and The American Ornithologists' Union, Washington, DC, U.S.A.

Tausch, R. J. 1999. Historic pinyon and juniper woodland development. Pages 12–19 in S. B. Monsen and R. Stevens (Compilers), Proceedings: ecology and management of pinyon–juniper communities within the interior West. Proceedings RMRS-P-9. USDA Forest Service, Rocky Mountain Research Station, Ogden, UT U.S.A.

Tausch R. J., N. E. West, and A. A. Nabi. 1981. Tree age dominance patterns in Great Basin pinyon–juniper woodlands. Journal of Range Management 34:259–264.

Trexel, D. R., R. N. Rosenfield, J. Bielefeldt, and E. A. Jacobs. 1999. Comparative nest site habitats in Sharp-shinned and Cooper's Hawks in Wisconsin. Wilson Bulletin 111:7–14.

USGS National Gap Analysis Program. 2004. Provisional digital land cover map for the southwestern United States. Version 1.0. RS/GIS Laboratory, College of Natural Resources, Utah State University, Logan, UT U.S.A.

Wiens, J. D., R. T. Reynolds, and B. R. Noon. 2006. Juvenile movement and natal dispersal of Northern Goshawks in Arizona. Condor 108:253–269.

Woodbridge, B., and P. J. Detrich. 1994. Territory occupancy and habitat patch size of Northern Goshawks in the southern Cascades of California. Studies in Avian Biology 6:83–87.

Woodbridge, B., and C. D. Hargis. 2006. Northern Goshawk inventory and monitoring technical guide. General Technical Report WO-71. USDA Forest Service, Washington, DC, U.S.A.

**ACCIPITER BROADCAST SURVEY FORM**

ROUTE DATA: Observer: _C K_ Date: _5/7/07_ General Location: _Wagon Ridge (P.B.)_
Route Start Pt: _1079_ End Pt: _1130_ Route Start Time: _10:20_ End Time: _14:40_
Weather Conditions (i.e., temp., cloud cover, wind): _Sunny, cool, light breeze_

STATION RESPONSE DATA: Species Responding: _CoHA_ Age: _U_ Sex: _U_
Time of Response: _10:55_ Time Elapsed Since First Broadcast: _~30 sec_
Broadcast Prior to Response (circle one): SSHA / (COHA) / NOGH
Response Type (circle one): (Call) / Call and Approach / Call and Fly-By / Silent Approach / Silent Fly-By
Estimated Distance to Response: _~400 m_ Estimated Bearing to Response: _40°_
Station Number: _1100_ Easting: _____ Northing: _____
General Habitat Description: _good, contiguous surrounding PJ, which appears_
_to get smaller and more open in direction of response_
Comments (e.g., observer confidence in species classification, distance and bearing, etc.): _responded to_
_all 4 COHA broadcasts, but response distant → conf. spp, less dist + bea_

STATION RESPONSE DATA: Species Responding: _____ Age: _____ Sex: _____
Time of Response: _____ Time Elapsed Since First Broadcast: _____
Broadcast Prior to Response (circle one): SSHA / COHA / NOGH
Response Type (circle one): Call / Call and Approach / Call and Fly-By / Silent Approach / Silent Fly-By
Estimated Distance to Response: _____ Estimated Bearing to Response: _____
Station Number: _____ Easting: _____ Northing: _____
General Habitat Description: _____
_____
Comments (e.g., observer confidence in species classification, distance and bearing, etc.): _____
_____

STATION RESPONSE DATA: Species Responding: _____ Age: _____ Sex: _____
Time of Response: _____ Time Elapsed Since First Broadcast: _____
Broadcast Prior to Response (circle one): SSHA / COHA / NOGH
Response Type (circle one): Call / Call and Approach / Call and Fly-By / Silent Approach / Silent Fly-By
Estimated Distance to Response: _____ Estimated Bearing to Response: _____
Station Number: _____ Easting: _____ Northing: _____
General Habitat Description: _____
_____
Comments (e.g., observer confidence in species classification, distance and bearing, etc.): _____
_____

**Figure A1.** Example accipiter broadcast survey data sheet. See the methods section for a detailed overview of the survey protocol.

## ACCIPITER NEST VEGETATION DATA

Date: 7/21/07   Surveyors: James C. + Rob S.   Accipiter Nest Species: NOGH

Nest Name: BLM 189   Easting: 〰   Northing: 〰   Elevation: 2135 m

Stand/Habitat Description: predominantly pinyon pine stand; to east area drops off into valley w/ younger P-J; bitterbrush large in area large opening ~30m away dominated by bitterbrush × gas well nearby – well used road ~120m from nest

| TREE SPP. | 3-8 cm | 8-15 cm | 15-23 cm | 23-38 cm | 38-53 cm | 53-69 cm | 69-84 cm | 84-102 cm | >102 cm |
|---|---|---|---|---|---|---|---|---|---|
| Live Pinyon | | I | II | HH II | II | | | | |
| Live Juniper | | II | | IIII | I | | | | |
| Live Other | | | | | | | | | |
| Dead Pinyon | | | I | | | | | | |
| Dead Juniper | | | I | | | | | | |
| Dead Other | | | | | | | | | |
| Pinyon Sapling | HH HH HH | | | | | | | | |
| Juniper Sapling | III | | | | | | | | |
| Other Sapling | | | | | | | | | |
| Downed Logs (≥1.5m long) | HH IIII | | | | | | | | |
| | | | | | | | | | |

### SHRUBS (# intersected by outstretched arms along transect)

| Dominant Species: | Live: HH HH | Live: HH HH III |
|---|---|---|
| bitterbrush | Dead: I | Dead: |

### PHOTOGRAPHS  Rob's cam
Nest: 206, 207, 209
Nest Area: 208
Nest tree: 210

### CANOPY
Max. height: 9.2 m
Min. height: 1.2 m

### NEST
Height: 4.7 cm
Width: 11.8 cm   Depth: 11.8 cm

### CAN. COVER

| | |
|---|---|
| 0 | I |
| 0 | 0 |
| I | 0 |
| I | 0 |
| I | I |

| | |
|---|---|
| I | I |
| I | I |
| 0 | 0 |
| I | I |

### GROUND COVER

| | |
|---|---|
| 0 | I |
| 0 | I |
| I | 0 |
| 0 | 0 |
| I | 0 |

| | |
|---|---|
| I | I |
| 0 | 0 |
| 0 | I |
| 0 | 0 |
| 0 | 0 |

### NEST TREE
Tr. Species: Pinyon Pine
Tr. Height: 7.9 m
Nest Height (in tree): 5.5 m
Min. Canopy Height: 1.2 m
Nest Tree and Nest Description: Live pinyon nest in crotch, somewhat exposed nest accessible by climbing

large amt of debris below nest adult feathers below nest; egg shell fragments below & inside nest.

**Figure A2.** Example vegetation survey data sheet used at 0.04-ha plots centered on accipiter nests. See the methods section for a detailed overview of the survey protocol.

**Figure B1.** Photograph of typical Sharp-shinned Hawk nesting area in the Piceance Basin, Colorado. The nest is indicated with an arrow.

**Figure B2.** Photograph of typical Cooper's Hawk nesting area in the Piceance Basin, Colorado. The nest is indicated with an arrow.

**Figure B3.** Photograph of typical Northern Goshawk nesting area in the Piceance Basin, Colorado. The nest is indicated with an arrow.

**These five documents are an integrated series.**

| | |
|---|---|
| **BLM Technical Note 432** | Raptor Nesting Near Oil and Gas Development: An Overview of Key Findings and Implications for Management Based on Four Reports by Hawk Watch International |
| **BLM Technical Note 433** | An Assessment of the Effects of Oil and Gas Field Activities on Nesting Raptors in the Rawlins, Wyoming and Price, Utah Field Offices of the Bureau of Land Management |
| **BLM Technical Note 434** | Artificial Nest Structures as Mitigation for Natural-Gas Development Impacts to Ferruginous Hawks (Buteo regalis) in South-Central Wyoming |
| **BLM Technical Note 435** | Accipiter Use of Pinyon–Juniper Habitats for Nesting in Northwestern Colorado |
| **BLM Technical Note 436** | Recommendations for Improved Raptor Nest Monitoring in Association with Oil and Gas Development Activities |

www.ingramcontent.com/pod-product-compliance
Lightning Source LLC
Chambersburg PA
CBHW052024280526
45793CB00005B/1110